Rainforest

by Annabelle Lynch

9112000197583

First published in 2013 by
Franklin Watts
338 Euston Road
London
NW1 3BH

Franklin Watts Australia
Level 17/207 Kent Street
Sydney
NSW 2000

Picture credits: Abhindia/Shutterstock: front cover.
Ryan M Bolton/Shutterstock: 12-13. Dhoxax/Shutterstock: 21.
Evocation Images/Shutterstock: 9. Chris Fredriksson/Alamy: 6.
Huang Chi-Feng/Shutterstock: 10. Javaman/Shutterstock: 15.
Jeep2499/Shutterstock: 18. Nigel Pavitt/Alamy: 16. Dr Moreley
Read/Shutterstock: 4-5.

Every attempt has been made to clear copyright.
Should there be any inadvertent omission please
apply to the publisher for rectification.

A CIP catalogue record for this book is
available from the British Library.

Dewey number: 577.3'4

ISBN 978 1 4451 1645 7(hbk)
ISBN 978 1 4451 1651 8 (pbk)
Library eBook ISBN 978 1 4451 2550 3

Series Editor: Julia Bird
Picture Researcher: Diana Morris
Series Advisor: Catherine Glavina
Series Designer: Peter Scoulding

Printed in China

Franklin Watts is a division of Hachette Children's Books,
an Hachette UK company.
www.hachette.co.uk

Contents

The words in **bold** can be found in the glossary.

What is a rainforest?

Rainforest is very thick forest with tall trees. It is found in places where there is a lot of rain.

The biggest rainforest is the Amazon is in South America.

Plant paradise

Plants grow well where it is warm and wet. Lots of different plants are found in the rainforest.

This rainforest flower is over a metre wide!

Up in the air

Tall trees make a leafy **shelter** over the rainforest. This is called the **canopy**.

Lots of animals live in the canopy because there is plenty of food there.

Down on the ground

The floor of the rainforest is dark and damp. Few plants live here because there is little light.

Leaves **rot** quickly on the rainforest floor.

Big bugs

The rainforest is home to millions of kinds of bugs.

This giant centipede eats lizards, frogs and mice.

Some are very small.
Some are very big!

Animals

Tigers, snakes and elephants all live in the rainforest. **Orang-utans** swing in the trees.

Orang-utans have long arms to reach for branches.

Rainforest people

People live in the rainforest, too. Their homes, food and clothes are all made using **materials** from the rainforest.

People have lived in the rainforest for thousands of years.

Food and medicine

The rainforest is important. It gives us food to eat. Many **medicines** also come from plants found in the rainforest.

Fruits such as bananas and mangoes grow in the rainforest.

Precious place

In some places, the rainforest is being cut down. We must protect it because it is home to so many people, animals and plants.

Maybe one day you will see the rainforest for yourself.

Glossary

Canopy – a shelter created by the leaves of tall trees

Material – something that something else is made from, such as wood

Medicine – something given to a person who is ill to make them better

Orang-utan – a large ape with orange fur and long arms

Rot – when something goes bad

Shelter – a cover

Websites:

http://www.rainforest-alliance.org.uk/kids

http://kids.mongabay.com/

Quiz

Use the information in the book to answer these questions.

1. Where is the biggest rainforest in the world?

2. What is the canopy?

3. Name an animal that swings in the rainforest trees.

4. How long have people lived in the rainforest?

5. Name a fruit that grows in the rainforest.

6. Why must we look after the rainforest?

(The answers are on page 24.)

Answers

1. South America
2. A leafy shelter
3. Orang-utans
4. For thousands of years
5. Bananas or mangoes
6. Because it is home to many people, animals and plants

Index